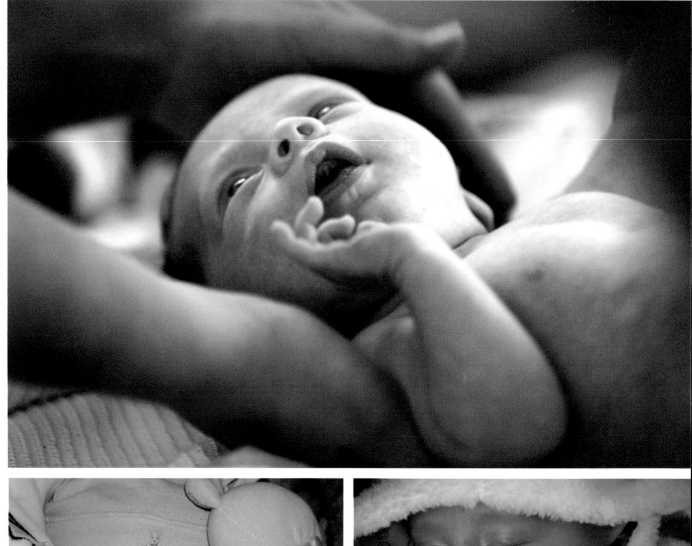

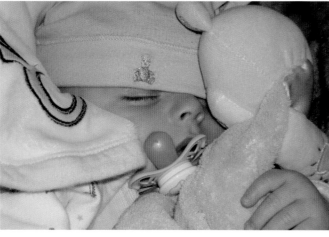

Shoot the Baby

Great baby photos and how to take them

Helen Webb

Vero Press

Vero Press

Shoot the Baby
Published by Vero Press
© Vero Press, 2011
First published 2011

A CIP catalogue record for this book is available from the British Library.
ISBN 978-0-9568422-0-6

Vero Press
26, High Street
Rickmansworth
Herts
WD3 1ER
UK

www.veropress.co.uk

Important Note from the Publisher
The information contained within this book was obtained by Vero Press from sources believed by us to be reliable. However, while every effort has been made to ensure its accuracy, no responsibility for loss or injury whatsoever occasioned to any person acting or refraining from action as a result of information contained herein can be accepted by the author or publisher.

All quotations remain the intellectual property of their respective originators. We do not assert any claim of copyright for individual quotations nor do we state our guarantee of their provenance. By quoting authors we do not in any way mean to imply their endorsement or approval of our book or its contents.

A list of all professional photography credits can be found on the inside back cover.

Vero Press is a trading name of Webb Strategy Ltd.
Printed in the UK.
Designed and typeset by AM Design; www.amdesigner.co.uk.

Contents

1. Top ten tips 3

2. Planning 9

3. Technique 19

4. Lighting 27

5. Composition 39

6. Props 51

7. A willing child 59

8. Smile, please 67

9. Finishing touches 71

10. The professionals 81

The subject matters 88

Spot the difference 122

Jargon buster 132

Bright colours help convey fun and energy, whereas neutral shades convey peace and gentleness.

Introduction

You're taking endless pictures of your baby, but they don't do justice to your bundle of joy. You want to capture their precious first smile, tooth and steps. But you're also trying to get your head around feeding, nappies, teething and colic. Things that used to take minutes seem to take hours. Oh, and you're sleep-deprived.

Shoot the Baby is a 'read while you feed' book. Simple, sound, practical advice that will improve your photos without taxing your brain. It's more about what you do than what the camera does, because good pictures are taken by people, not cameras.

Most of the advice in the book applies equally to digital or film photographers although I have assumed you are using a digital camera. Most of the pictures in the book have been taken by amateurs, on a range of cameras from digital SLRs to mobile phones. They are not perfect shots, but help demonstrate how to take the 'hit and miss' out of the 'point and shoot'.

"Tired babies aren't the greatest smilers." "Always have a spare battery with you." Tips like these may sound obvious, but they should help you avoid making simple but frustrating mistakes. It's beyond irritating to arrive at the Christening, only to find your camera is as low on battery and memory space as you are!

I have it on good authority that parents of baby boys find it odd to read "her" in the text and vice versa. After much debate we have gone with the inelegant "they". Apologies go to Miss Packer, who taught me English Grammar at school.

'A word in grey' denotes a word which is explained in the 'jargon buster' at the back of the book.

I wish you the best of luck with your photography and hope this book leads to a more enjoyable and rewarding experience behind the lens.

Helen Webb

Acknowledgements

I would like to thank the following people who helped immensely in the production of this book. Jonathan Ray, Harriet Webb, Helen Randle, Sue Lacey, William Lack, Louise Spilsbury and 'the girlies' for their advice and guidance, Andy Magee for his design expertise, my husband Quentin for his endless patience and my family for love and laughter over the years.

Most thanks are due of course to my friends, Alison Parker, Amanda Allan, Andy Magee, Carly Trisk-Grove, Chris Buchanan, Emma Gordon, Ishanthi Bratby, Jane Price-Hunt, Kathy Allan, Kelly Patterson, Lisa Thompson, Marius Franek, Richard Stacy, Sophie Baker, Sue Lacey, Sylvaine Malialis and Veronique Robinson for their pictures - and to the beautiful babies in the images, without whom there would be no book.

For Oakley, my inspiration...

10% of all profits from the sale of this book will be donated to the Family Holiday Association, which works tirelessly to help children smile through the toughest of situations.

"You don't take a photograph,
you make it." – Ansel Adams

Top ten tips

If you consistently follow these ten super-simple rules and these ten super-simple rules only, your pictures – and baby – will stand out from the crowd:

1. De-clutter your shots. A camera won't filter out irrelevant details as your brain does. Watch out especially for washing, dirty plates or anything behind your baby's head. Move yourself, the baby or the mess, until the shot is clutter-free.

2. Take a step closer. Or crop the shot later. Remember, there's no pavement in the Mona Lisa. As a simple rule, try to fill two thirds of the shot with your subject.

3. Bin most of your pictures. To improve your photography instantly, simply delete the bad ones! No professional will show you everything they took.

4. Know your camera. Those buttons are there for a reason. Read the manual, then venture beyond the fully automatic (usually green) setting. For each shot, take one on fully automatic and one with the new setting, then spot the difference.

5. Personality shots. All babies smile and all smiling babies are gorgeous. But don't forget to capture the serious, sad, cross and tired looks – to help you remember all those quirky little mannerisms.

6. Consider the light. The light in a photo is as important as the subject. Look for the direction and quality of your light source and use natural light (not flash) whenever possible.

7. Landscape or portrait. Don't be afraid to turn the camera around into the upright (portrait) position. It's surprisingly good for ... portraits!

8. Experiment. Take shots from different angles (above, below, at a level), at different times of day and on different settings. Try to remember or record what you did when, so you can repeat the shots you like.

9. Have a laugh. Relax and your baby will too. Say something stupid or unexpected. Blow a raspberry. Encourage silly behaviour. Smile a lot – it's infectious.

10. Print or upload your photos. Is your computer a photo graveyard? Share your best shots with family and friends by uploading or printing your pictures. There are many great photo sharing websites, but remember that grandparents still love the sort that go in a frame on top of the TV.

"Photographers deal in things which are continually vanishing and when they have vanished, there is no contrivance on earth can make them come back again." – Henri Cartier-Bresson

Planning

Be prepared, whether you're setting up a shoot, or seizing a spontaneous moment.

Expect to work a little to get a great picture. A key difference between the amateur and the professional photographer is that a professional will plan the lighting, props, timing, style and composition, whereas an amateur will often grab the camera, press the button and expect perfection.

Have a camera with you as often as possible. "You should have seen the one that got away" applies to photos as well as fish. If you do forget your camera, remember you can probably use your mobile phone.

Always have a spare battery with you. On digital cameras, both the display panel and flash devour power.

Check you have a memory card and that it has plenty of space on it. And always carry a spare.

Be ready. Even taking off the lens cap and turning on the camera can take long enough to miss the moment.

Photography is the ultimate fad. You take eighty shots in a week, then none for ages. Take a few shots on your baby's monthly anniversary to capture every stage of their development (e.g. 20th of each month if your baby is born on 20th).

Which style of image are you after? Have
a look through magazines or websites for
inspiration when planning your shoot.

Think about your location, especially once the baby
is walking. Beaches (early in the morning), gardens,
woods and fields all make great backdrops for a toddler.

Pick your spot. Where will the light come from? How
clear is the background? Does it need any "arranging"?

Take pictures of your baby in familiar environments e.g.
in a favourite park, in your garden, in their bedroom.
They will love looking back in years to come.

Think about your location, especially once the baby is walking. Beaches, gardens, woods and fields all make great backdrops.

Photograph your baby in the same location on their first birthday, then fifth, tenth etc. The consistency of the backdrop (e.g. a Christmas tree) will emphasise the changes in your child.

Try some photo journalism; a sequence of pictures which tells a story. Maybe the baby's day, from first stretches to tucked up for the night. Or your baby sitting looking at an object, starting to crawl towards the object, reaching the object and smiling back at you as they hold the object. Grouped together, such shots are called a **story board**.

Indoors, try using a white or black sheet for a clean background. And a pale, fluffy rug (or sheepskin) gives a nice bit of texture. To highlight a face, use a black background and dark clothes or a white background and white clothes.

If you're struggling to find an uncluttered spot in the house, try the stairs.

Make sure you are in some of the shots. At the time, you may think you look awful, but years later you will regret your apparent absence from your baby's early years. If necessary, use your camera's **self-timer**.

Time the shoot carefully. When is best for
the baby and when is best for the light?

Which props would you like in the shot
and which props do you need out of
the shot? See page 51 for ideas.

Get everything ready in advance or your baby's
attention span will run out just as you're sorted.
Guaranteed. Have someone else around to help.
All the best photographers have assistants.

Set up a photo session with friends, perhaps from
your antenatal class. It's more fun, more likely
to happen and easier to manage as a team.

Plan what your baby will wear, avoiding
distracting motifs and patterns.
And always pack a spare set!

Unless the snotty look is the one
you are after, wipe your baby's
nose before you shoot.

If you can spare a few pounds, buy
yourself a mini **tripod**. Set up the shot, then
stand to the side engaging the baby.

Consider buying a lightweight folding daylight
reflector. They are cheap to buy, easy to
use and vastly improve the lighting.

"It is a matter of putting your brain, your eye and your heart in the same line of sight." – Henri Cartier-Bresson

Technique

**Rules are there to be broken, but
they're a useful starting point.**

Move and shoot, rather than 'point and shoot'.
Walk around your subject to find the best angle.

Whenever possible, bring the baby to the camera
not the other way around. Choose a good location
and you'll get better composed, better lit images.

To avoid **camera shake**, brace yourself against
a wall or post, stand with your feet apart,
hold your elbows against your sides and
breathe out slowly as you take the shot.

If your camera has a range of settings, use them.

🐦 Highlight your subject by using the portraiture setting, which is generally a picture of a head. This will focus on your subject and slightly blur the background. (A short **depth of field**.)

🌷 The 'macro' or flower setting helps you get right up close to details of your own little flower (for example, fingers and toes.) Take care, however - only the elements highlighted by a green box or flashing blocks (on your viewfinder or display panel) will be in focus.

[☺] If your camera has **face detection**, switch it on. It will put a box around the face it will focus on. Some cameras are even clever enough to take the photo only when the subject smiles.

For other cameras, use the **focus lock** to avoid blurred subjects. Most cameras still focus on the dead centre of the viewfinder. This could be the gap between two people, leaving your subjects blurry and the background crisp. Learn how to use the **focus lock** to keep off centre subjects in focus. It takes a bit of getting used to, but really is worth practising until you get the hang of it.

If you have a **zoom lens**, use it. The further back you are, the less intrusive you will be. And the longer lens will tend to blur backgrounds, so the child stands out more. To keep the features in proportion, try not to zoom beyond 105mm.

On a compact digital camera, there are often two parts to the zoom. Listen for the lens moving – if the lens is not moving, the 'zoom' is simply re-cropping your shot (and reducing the image quality).

Take a series of shots in quick succession to capture a range of expressions. Your camera may have a continual shooting mode to help you.

Focus on the eyes. You can get away
with slightly blurred hands or hair but
the eyes should always be sharp.

When photographing a moving child, use your
focus lock to focus on one spot and press
the **shutter release** as the child reaches it.

Learn to anticipate. Some digital cameras
have a slight delay, which can be infuriating
with children, who move so fast and
change mood so quickly. To help reduce
the effect when shooting multiple shots,
try a **high speed memory card**.

If your camera gives a **shutter speed**, be careful below 1/125 of a second. You might not move, but the child probably will.

For most shots, crouch down to baby level.

Take plenty. Professionals would never expect every shot to be good and would usually take at least five for every one they keep. If in doubt, keep snapping.

Save a couple of shots for when your subjects think you've finished. A trick used by Lord Lichfield at Prince Charles and Lady Diana's wedding to get a really relaxed shot of even the most formal grouping.

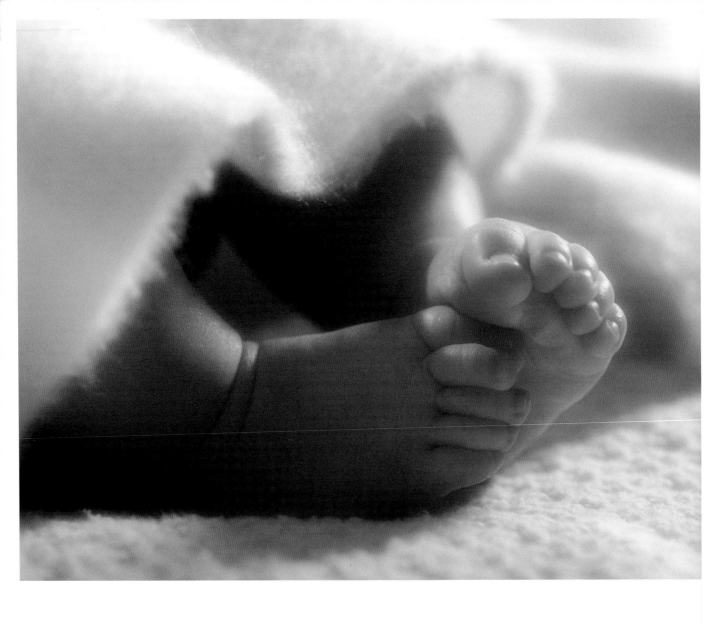

"Photography is the art of writing with light."
– Gerardo Suter

Lighting

Let there be light. And let it fall gently across my baby's face to create the perfect picture.

Good lighting will greatly improve your photography. Think about where it is coming from. Is there enough or too much? What shadows does it cast? We usually take light for granted, so it takes quite a bit of practice to understand how it will affect your shots. Experiment to become light aware.

If in doubt, ensure the main light source is in front of your subject – especially if you have a fidgety child.

For more interesting shots, position the child so the light hits them at an angle (45 degrees works well). To try this out, find a tree where one side is lighter than the other. Stand someone on the light side and gradually turn their head towards you until half their face is in light and half in shadow.

Try backlighting your child for a "halo" effect.

When the main light is behind the child (for example, a child standing in a doorway), you'll probably need flash, a lamp or a **reflector** to light their face and hence reduce **contrast** or shadows.

An hour after dawn and an hour before sunset
are the best times for a soft, warm, natural
light. Afternoon light will boost colour; early
morning light will reduce its intensity.

Avoid bright sunlight. It creates deep
shadows, **contrast** and squints! Children
squint into the sun even more than adults
as their eyes are more sensitive.

If the light is too bright, wait for a cloud, find some
shade or get someone to hold something out of
shot above the child's head (to block some light).

Check if any shadows appear in the
viewfinder – including your own,
which should not be in the shot.

Shadows reveal shape on a face. You need
some, but you don't want too many. At midday,
when the sun is overhead, the eye sockets end
up very dark (too much **contrast**). Turn on your
flash (or use a **reflector**) to lighten the eyes.

Don't be afraid to use light to create
silhouettes in your shots. The shape of a
toddler can be as appealing as the features.

Use natural
light as much
as possible.

Even indoors, use natural light as much as possible. Balance your camera on the edge of a table, then turn off the flash, using the "flash off" setting ⚡. Use white sheets or a **reflector** to throw even more light onto your subject. This works very well for sleeping babies, but not at all for wriggly toddlers.

At birthday parties, line up the shot so candles on a cake appear just underneath the child's chin. Turn off the flash (and use a **tripod**) so the candles really glow.

Avoid purely fluorescent lighting – it's unflattering.

Place your child next to a window (ideally
north facing) for a lovely soft, natural light.
Again, you may need to use something white
to reflect extra light onto your subject.

If you are using flash indoors, try not to place your
subject right in front of a wall, because you will get
a really harsh shadow. Move them forwards a little.

Don't point the flash directly at a mirror
or window - stand at an angle.

Most built-in flashes only work for two
to three metres. Grab front row seats
for success at the school play.

Move around until you can see little glints of light in your baby's eyes. These 'catch lights' will make your baby's eyes twinkle.

To avoid **red eye**:

- Get your subject to look at your shoulder rather than directly into the camera.

- Turn on all the room lights.

- Use a daylight or energy efficient light bulb in the room.

- As a last resort, use the **red-eye** reduction 👁 setting on your camera (or correct it using **photo editing software**).

If you have a Program ("P") mode, try using it as your default setting. The main difference between this setting and fully automatic is that, with this setting, you control the flash. Using the "P" mode will force you to be conscious of the light.

Move around until you can see little glints of light in your baby's eyes. These 'catch lights' will make your baby's eyes twinkle.

If you have the luxury of a multi-directional or off-camera (posh) flash unit, bounce the flash from a white ceiling or wall to diffuse the light.

Check out how to change the 'film' speed (ISO) on your camera, as this is one of the easiest ways to alter the light in the shot. If there's not enough natural light, try increasing the ISO number to avoid using flash. But be aware that the higher the ISO, the grainier the shot.

"I'm always mentally photographing
everything as practice." – Minor White

Composition

A well-composed shot is more in your control than a well-composed child! Choose your subject matter carefully, then decide how to arrange them within the shot.

Snap then circle. Take one shot to avoid missing the moment, then walk round the baby to see if there's a better angle.

Decide if you want to be above your subject looking down, below them looking up or on a level with them. Experiment – you will get very different results.

Make sure there is nothing crucial on the absolute edge of the viewfinder or display panel.

Distraction or narration? Is the digger in the background unnecessary clutter or your toddler's latest obsession? Check that each element of the shot adds to the story you're telling.

Strong lines can help structure a shot – especially diagonal lines, which lead your eye to, or with, the subject. If there's a path in the shot, move until it cuts across your viewfinder on the diagonal.

Repeated forms, such as steps, railings or bubbles, also make a good backdrop.

Use natural shapes to frame a child's face, such as the handle of a pram, the rungs of a ladder, an archway or the branches of a tree.

Strong lines can help
structure a shot – especially
diagonal lines, which lead
your eye to, or with,
the subject.

Consider the colour in the shot. Bright colours help convey fun and energy, whereas neutral shades convey peace and gentleness – so photograph your baby in the cot and the toddler in the ball pool.

Don't always include the whole scene. Leaving some things to the imagination can make a powerful and interesting image. Tottering legs (without the rest of the body), maybe, or a group of toddlers enthralled by a magic show (which is out of shot).

Don't include other people's children in your pictures without permission (even in the background). Be especially careful on the beach.

If it's a choice between lots of grass
or lots of sky in the shot, in general go
for the sky. A thin strip of light at the top
of the picture can be distracting.

Compose images to capture the magical
details of a newborn. Focus in on tiny
fingers, curled up toes, dimpled hands, long
eyelashes, rolls of fat or a quivering lip.

Use reflections and shadows to good
effect. Try taking a picture of the
shadow without the person – maybe
two children holding hands or a
child on Dad's shoulders.

Child photography, like sports photography, involves an unpredictable, moving target. Try to foresee where they'll go or what they'll do next and compose the shot in readiness. Easier said than done!

If you are taking a group, decide where you want them to look – all at the camera, all at each other or all at something else (but not all in different directions). Blow a few bubbles to draw everyone's attention to the same point.

If photographing a child in **profile** or part profile, show the space they are looking or walking into.

A stance or gesture can display mood and emotion just as effectively as the face itself. For an interesting image, compose the shot to capture your toddler's character without showing their facial features.

Position the baby just off centre for a more interesting **composition**. If you have the most important element of your picture (e.g. the eyes) about one third in from the top (or bottom) and one third in from one side of the viewfinder or display panel, you have achieved the 'rule of thirds' that professionals learn about at photography school.

Check nothing appears to be growing out of the baby's head.

Use natural shapes to frame a child's face.

For a classic portrait, fill at least two thirds of the frame with the child. However, this does not apply if the background is part of the story you are telling (known as an 'environmental' portrait).

Remove distractions before you take the photo. Glance across the whole viewfinder from corner to corner before you take the picture, watching for annoying shadows, dirty plates, telegraph poles and the like.

If there's a horizon, make sure it's straight – and not running through the child's head.

Don't **crop** at joints e.g. knees, elbows or ankles. It always looks odd.

Check the clothes as well as the expressions. A stained T-shirt or creased collar can ruin a shot – or take ages to correct on the computer.

When taking a family portrait, look at the outline formed by your group. Aim for a smooth (though not necessarily symmetrical) shape, by grouping people of similar height together.

Encouraging cuddles and kisses is a good way to ensure your subjects are really close together – and it will also help relax them.

Look through the 'subject matters' section of this book for compositions you might like to recreate yourself.

"Sometimes you can tell a large story with
a tiny subject." – Eliot Porter

Props

You'll probably need a cup of tea (or something stronger) at the end of a child's formal photo session. Other things to gather together include:

Favourite toys and teddies to use in the shot.

Unfamiliar toys and teddies to use out of the shot. Squeaking or moving parts are great for holding the baby's attention.

Food. Yoghurt, ice-cream or chocolate, to please the camera. And a favourite snack to please the toddler.

Things that are a bit too big for them – let toddlers wear your shoes or a hat over their eyes. Alternatively, sit them in a huge chair or cardboard box.

Nature; flowers, snow, water, sand, mud etc.

Pets.

Parents. Unlike teenagers, most babies will
visibly relax when a parent is close.

A pot of bubbles or a bunch of balloons.

A book or game to distract them from the camera.

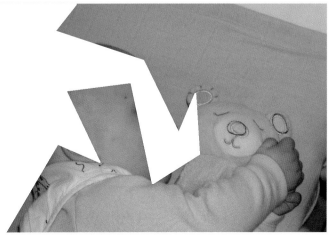

Things they aren't usually allowed
– your glasses or keys maybe.

A 'size marker' to give a sense of scale,
especially for tiny newborns. Put their hand
in your hand or place a tape measure or
pencil somewhere in the shot (being sure
the baby doesn't grab it, of course).

Make up. Even very young girls love putting
on lipstick in front of a mirror and their
concentration will ensure a natural pose.

Something new or mysterious– carved pumpkins, birthday cake etc. Beware: babies often try to grab the candle flame on their first birthday cake.

Glasses without the lenses in, to highlight their eyes.

Some padding or a pillow inside the pram to ensure more light hits your baby's face.

Trees. They are great for leaning on or hiding behind – and there's usually one close by.

Things you might need in between shots – a
muslin, snacks, spare clothes, patience.

A balloon to put on your shoulder or something
interesting to put at your height on a shelf behind
you. This will ensure the baby looks up, not down.

A large, empty picture frame to crawl through,
peep through, hide behind and generally have
fun with. (Pick one up at a car boot sale.)

Your "thing". A football scarf, paintbrush or
computer to create that cute "mini-me" portrait.

Unlike teenagers, most babies will visibly relax when a parent is close.

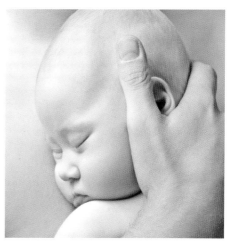

"It is more important to click with people than
to click the shutter." – Alfred Eisenstaedt

A willing child

**Burping, whistling, talking gobbledygook
and bribery are all accepted photographers'
tactics to keep a child willing and relaxed.
Plan your method in advance.**

Think about the time of day. When is best for your
baby? Immediately after a sleep is generally a good
time - tired babies aren't the greatest smilers.

Let them wear clothes (or a costume)
they are comfortable in, but be aware that
bright colours can reflect onto the baby's
face. Avoid bright green T-shirts.

Don't make a big deal of it. Try to
ensure they don't notice you.

Stalk the child! Let the toddler lead you to the funny shot as they put things on their heads, step into puddles and so on. Learn the patience of an undercover agent.

Hook your keys over the end of an elongated metal coat hanger to direct a baby's gaze.

Stick a bright sticker on the front of your camera and bring it to the child's attention. This can be a risky strategy – many toddlers will lunge at the camera to peel it off.

Give them something to concentrate on. A distracted child is nearly as good as a willing one.

Ask them what they can hear. Focus their attention on traffic noise, bird song, a ticking clock or an imaginary cat for a pensive look and a moment's concentration.

Allow toddlers to clamber over furniture they wouldn't usually. Let them bounce on the bed or climb on the sofa.[1]

Encourage toddlers to exaggerate what they are doing – a silly look or walk, maybe. This will relax them and take their attention away from the camera.

1. While making sure they are safe at all times, as my editor so rightly points out.

Play a game with them – crawling along
the floor towards each other, peeping
behind curtains or hide and seek.

Ask them to wink, point or wave at you. Demonstrate
what you want them to do and they will usually copy.

Take photos of something else and use the toddler
as an assistant, at first behind the lens, then
gradually in front of the lens. For example, take
pictures of a favourite toy and then ask your child
to help you by holding it in a particular way.

Set a timer for a shoot with a toddler. Give each other ten minutes. They co-operate with you for ten minutes and then you play whatever game they want to for ten minutes. (Never the other way around!)

If your toddler fidgets, ask them to cross their legs or tuck one leg under the other. Occupy their fingers by giving them something to hold, folding their arms or resting their head in their hands.

With toddlers, if in doubt, bribe them!

If the toddler absolutely won't play ball at an important moment (e.g. a family portrait) try the following:

• Encourage them and others to pull a funny or grumpy face.

• Give them a hat to wear, pulled down over their eyes.

• Allow them to sit with their back to the photographer. The chances are they will glance round. If they don't, say "all finished" and take the picture when they turn.

• If all else fails, allow them not to be in the shot but put something in the shot to represent them. A favourite teddy or just their shoes.

"Photography has no rules. It is not a sport. It is the result which counts, no matter how it is achieved." – Bill Brandt

Smile, please

Throw sanity and caution to the wind. Abandon your credibility to capture that toothy (or toothless!) grin.

Shoot them as they wake in the morning!

Play peek-a-boo. This is particularly good around the time of their first tooth.

Use a puppet, squeaky toy or bubbles.

Make a noise, blow a raspberry or say something stupid.

Sneeze – babies seem to think it's
funny, especially if it's loud.

Tickle the baby with a (clean!) long-reach duster.

Ask an adult to lift the baby up over their head.
It's a great 'relationship' shot and the baby
will usually beam on the third or fourth lift.

Get someone to stand directly
behind you, pulling faces.

Have a really good laugh yourself.

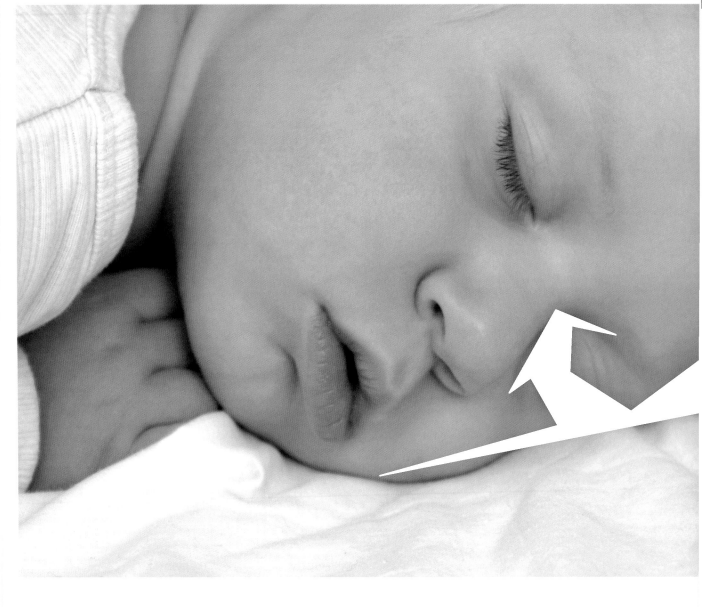

"What you have caught on film is captured forever...
it remembers little things, long after you have
forgotten everything." – Aaron Siskind

Finishing touches

The more you take, the more you have to organise. Sort as you go, or you'll end up with a hard disk or drawer full of unsorted, unnamed, unseen photos.

Only keep good or unique images. This is very important. It makes you look a much better photographer and saves embarrassment all round.

Bin the rest. This will result in a more manageable number of shots that you might actually look at. De-clutter, feng shui and all that.

Set up folders on your computer and rename shots regularly (at least once a month). If you don't, you will gradually take fewer and fewer shots because you can't face the filing.

Create a filing system and stick to it, remembering that the computer will sort the files in numeric and then alphabetic order. Filing by year and month is a good approach. Keep a number at the front of the file name to label shots in terms of content, while storing them in date order (e.g. Img_2015.jpg becomes 2015first_steps.jpg).

Back up your files regularly, ideally on an external hard drive. Keep printed copies of the best images, in case of total digital meltdown. Don't put it off – those pictures of your baby really are irreplaceable.

Try a little digital enhancement using **post-production** software such as Adobe® Photoshop® or similar. You don't want to spend your life at a computer, but good **cropping** and **red eye** removal is usually worth it.

If you edit a photo, save it as a separate file, so the original remains intact. Always work from the original, because every time you alter a digital image, a little image quality is lost.

Don't forget black and white. You can change from colour to black and white when editing – which is better than doing it on camera. (Look out for the editing option 'desaturate'.)

Using **post-production** software, you can change the brightness and colour balance of your image, remove unsightly objects and much more. Ask someone you know to give you a demonstration, or find an online video tutorial to guide you through the tools.

Once a year, put the top twenty shots of your baby into a separate folder. Or choose one from each month of the year and make a calendar.

Select your best shots and have them printed professionally (online or on the High Street). Few home printers get such good results.

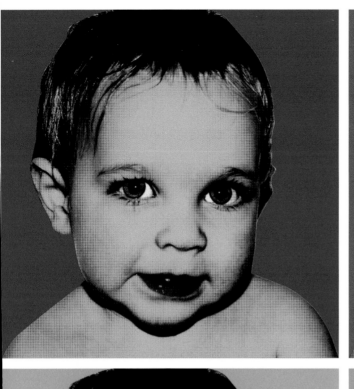
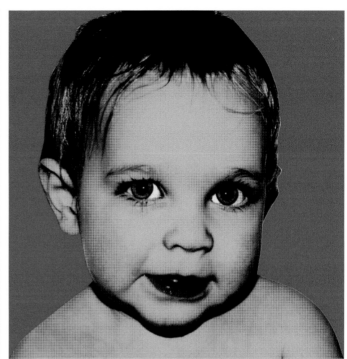
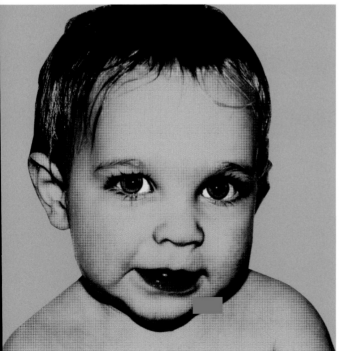
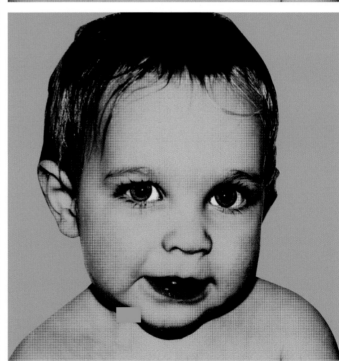

In processing shops, look out for the self-service machines where you can change the format, remove **red eye**, **crop** and print the shots yourself.

Decide on your printing preference and stick to it, so you can mix and match pictures at a later date. Gloss or matt. Borders or plain. 18cm x 13cm (7" x 5") or 15cm x 10cm (6" x 4").

Ask your photo processing shop if they have a baby club offering discounts or free product.

Consider making a photo book. (Type 'photo book' into your internet search engine for many companies offering this service at low prices).

Use a photo sharing website to create online albums and to enable friends and family to view or order copies of your shots. Or, use your images to create a blog.

Never make naked shots of your child available on the internet, via a blog, photo sharing or social networking site.

Many digital photos are around 3 MB in size so you may not be able to email more than one or two at a time. To reduce the file size, reduce the size of the image, reduce the image quality, or 'zip' the file before sending it.

If you are hanging your pictures on the wall, think carefully about the type of frame and mount. Or would you prefer a canvas print with neither?

New 'special effects' websites are created almost daily, allowing you to turn your images into cartoons, Christmas cards, magazine covers and so on. You can add text, make a photo montage and see your baby as Andy Warhol would have. Search the internet for the latest 'fun photo editing websites'.

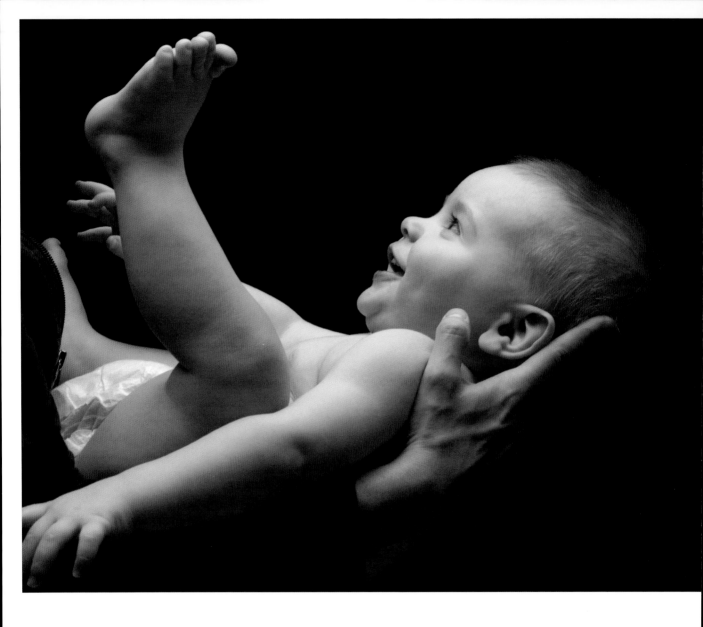

"It takes a lot of looking before you learn to see the extraordinary." – David Bailey

The professionals

However closely you follow the advice in this book, the professional will still have the edge in terms of experience – and equipment. A professional shoot is rarely cheap, but usually worth it.

Think about when you want to get a professional in. Popular times include:

- Pregnancy – a special time.

- Newborn – one to two weeks after birth. These are hard shots to take yourself as they will generally be inside and need careful lighting.

- First steps – book a professional session when your baby is just walking to capture those adorable, wobbly steps.

- Siblings – when number two is born.

Decide if you want the shots done in a studio, at home or 'on location', such as by your favourite duck pond or in Granny's garden?

Think about the photographic style you are after – traditional or contemporary, formal or informal? Do you want naked baby pictures or not? Many modern studios will take great, high energy shots, but be aware that this may involve images taken at an angle or with heads and feet cut off.

Check out the photographer's previous work. Do you like their style? Tell them which images particularly caught your eye so they understand your preferences.

Speak to the photographer's previous clients to know what to expect. Put the photographer's name into an internet search engine to see what people are saying about them (good or bad) online.

Check the photographer's pricing policy. Will they charge for the shoot and then for each image or are a number of shots included in the fee? What sizes of images are available? Never pay the entire amount up front.

How much **post-production** work is included in the fee? Many professionals will whiten teeth and smooth away skin blemishes. Is this what you want?

Don't book your session for a time when your baby will be hungry or tired.

Always speak to the photographer (not just the receptionist or assistant) before the shoot, as their personality is important. Do you click? Are they relaxed, patient, friendly?

Make sure you understand what will happen on the day. How much time will the photographer give you? How many shots will they take? What range of shots will be covered? How many will you see?

Ask what you should bring for you and the baby (clothes, toys etc.).

Check out practical details, such as what happens if the baby needs changing or feeding during the shoot.

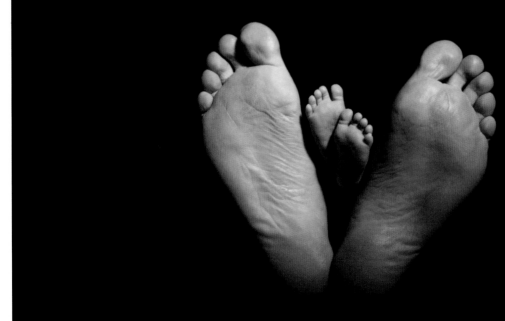

Check the timescales - especially if Christmas or family birthdays are coming up. When will you view and then receive the photos?

Remember that very few professional photographers will give you full quality digital copies of the images (or the negatives), although you can always ask.

The photographer almost always retains the intellectual property. This means that once you've signed the **model release form**, the photographer can re-use photos of your child. If this concerns you, discuss it with the photographer before the start of the session and read the form carefully before signing.

Birth

My world

Special people

Discovery

The subject matters

Milestones

Funny

Memories

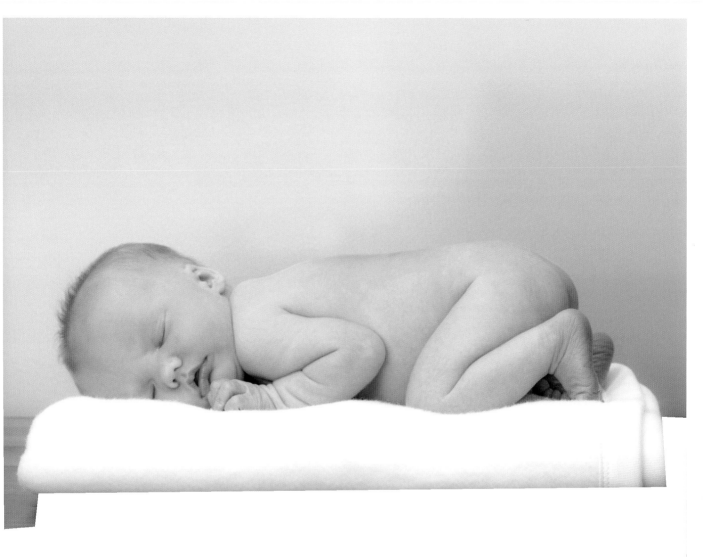

Recreate some of the following shots and send us
your own ideas at www.shootthebaby.co.uk.

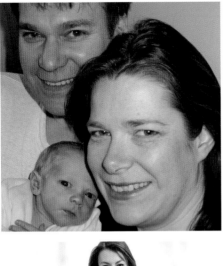

Birth

Demi Moore led the way and we must follow. Celebrate the bump. Bubble bath is subtle. An older sibling with the bump is also nice (hands on the bump, kissing the bump or even listening to the bump).

Pregnancy memories – eating the food you craved, doing yoga and so on.

Try to get a 'brand new baby' shot, just post delivery.

A tiny foot – or hand – held lovingly – or gripping your finger.

Use a soft light to capture the tiny, sleeping newborn.

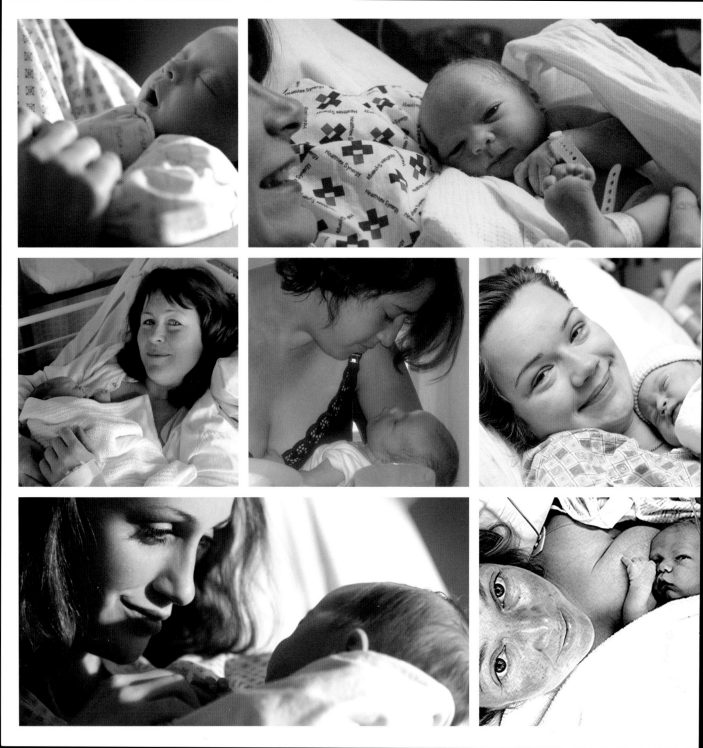

At the time, the birthing equipment seems incidental but years later these details will trigger the memories. A tag, the birthing pool, the ward name.

The easiest, most discreet position for a photographer to shoot a newborn feeding is over the mother's shoulder. Wait a few weeks until she is totally comfortable feeding – and being photographed.

Ask someone to take a family shot as early as possible – ideally within a week of the birth. Preferably by a window, with the flash off and the baby held right up close to your heads.

My world

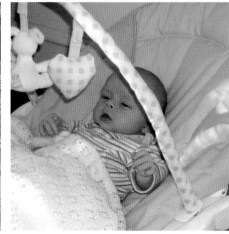

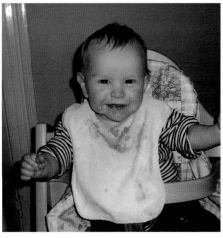

Children are always fascinated by the part of their lives they can't remember. Record their world – their bedroom, pram, favourite teddy, pet. The time they spent in the bath, the baby gym, the high chair, the garden and so on. Your local haunts, such as the local park, swimming pool or coffee shop.

Special people

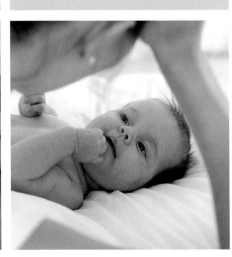

With Mum. Try a few different poses. Over Mum's shoulder is always popular. Or Mum and baby lying on their side, with Mum's face above the baby's. Or the baby lying down, with Mum bending over close to their head.

With Dad. Holding the baby or toddler above his head for great eye contact and laughter.

With their siblings. Back to back, in a tight hug, snuggling on the sofa or lying on their fronts. However they feel comfortable.

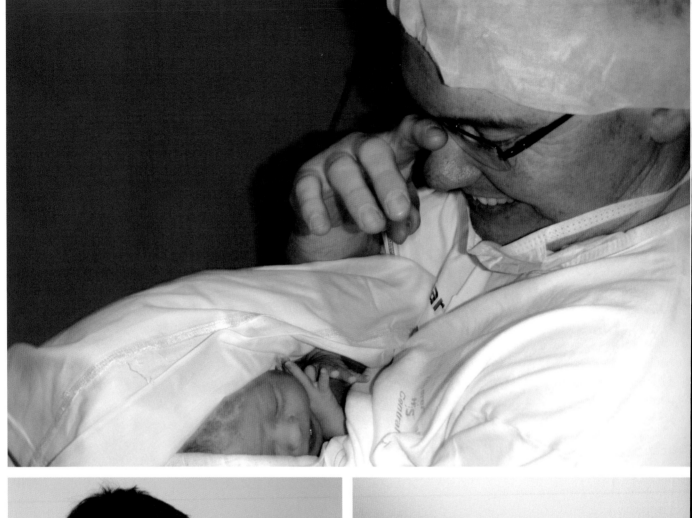

With grandparents. And, if you're
lucky, four generations.

With the midwife.

With the nanny, childminder or staff at the Nursery.

With the antenatal class babies.
Or with the children of your best friends
– there's a good chance they'll still
know each other in years to come.

With extended family and significant others.
For example, cousins and godparents.

Discovery

If you can, stand back and use a zoom lens so you don't break their concentration. Or position yourself behind the baby so you're not in their line of sight.

Sand. Great for sifting, digging - and eating! Shoot your child next to their name, scrawled in the sand, or make family footprints and write the year next to them. Have similar fun with the first experience of snow.

Food. The first taste of puréed vegetables – when the hand and spoon go in the mouth and the food is wiped around the outside!

Nothing beats a great splash
in a puddle with a toddler.

Flower. Or the first carved pumpkin. Children and nature. A winning combination.

Mirror. Use natural light or stand at an angle for this shot, so the flash doesn't bounce off the mirror. Place the mirror near natural light and test different angles. (For alternative reflections try a shiny table or a puddle).

Puddles. Nothing beats a great splash in a puddle with a toddler. Take a couple of shots, then put the camera down and join in the fun!

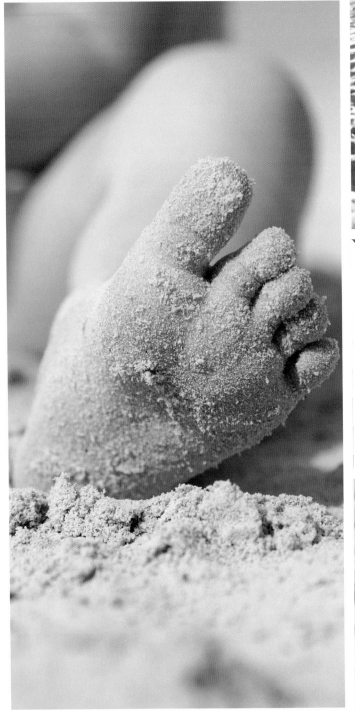

Fingers up noses. Once discovered,
never forgotten.

Make up. Children are the best
mimics. Which doesn't say much for
Mummy's skills with the lipstick.

Gravity. Apparently that phase where
they tip everything over the highchair
is 'discovering gravity' not 'discovering
disobedience'. Either way, it's a phase that
lasts long enough to capture for posterity.

Milestones

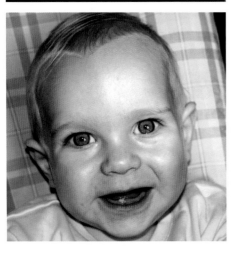

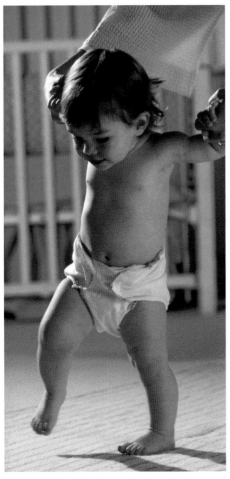

There are many milestones in a baby's first couple of years, so get snapping. Crawling, teething, cruising, walking. The first haircut, first shoes, first solid food, first set of wheels. Birthdays, Christmas, sitting on the potty and other momentous occasions.

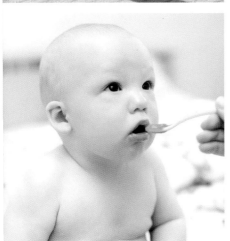

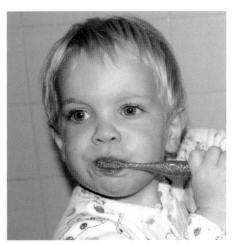

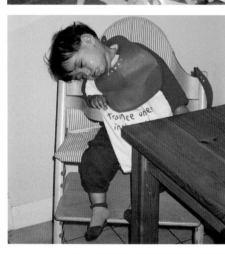

Funny

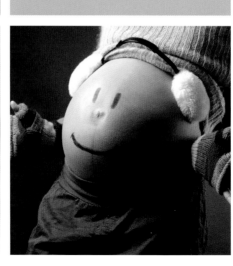

Although you may be able to pose some of these, many will be 'grab the moment' shots. You'll laugh at the images for years to come, even if they are a bit out of focus and not particularly well lit.

In anything oversized. Kids love trying out your clothes, shoes, hats and glasses. Or use large props like a big bed, chair or newspaper.

Naked, except the wellington boots. Or dungarees. Or hat. Or nappy. And make sure you capture those cute rolls of puppy fat and lovely baby dimples.

Pulling silly faces. Need I say more?

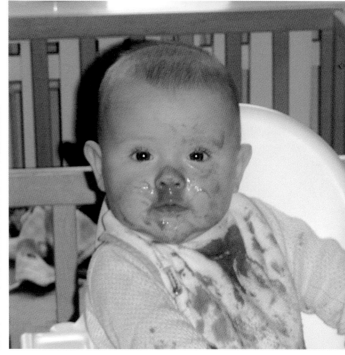
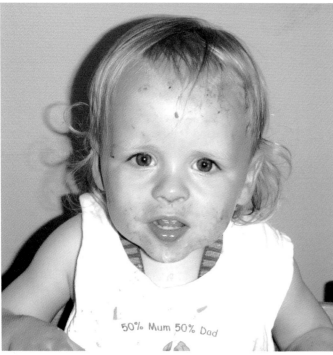

Grumpy – or even crying. It may not be funny at the time, but the 'stroppy poppy' phase is hilarious once it's over. Crop in close on these shots and use your portraiture setting to blur the background. When their world crumples, they are totally absorbed by their anguish – and we should be too!

Messy. Covered in ice-cream, mud, chocolate, yoghurt . Shots like this are always in good supply.

Having a laugh. Thow them up above
your head. Swing them high in the park.
Let them bounce on the bed.[2]

Favourite poses. Does your baby constantly
stick their head between their legs? Or play
peek-a-boo, peeping out from behind curtains
or bursting out of kitchen cupboards?

In a cardboard box. Or a washing basket.
Or a bucket (without the water!).

2. Without letting them fall off, of course.

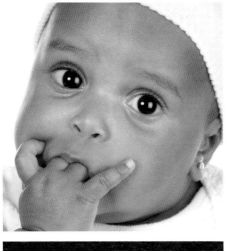

Memories

You think you'll never forget, but within a few years, you do. Does your baby sit for hours watching the washing machine? Walk around clutching breadsticks? Spend hours reading? Sit in the washing basket? Eat a favourite food? Always suck their fingers? Record those habits and gestures – in years to come you'll enjoy them together; remembering on your part and discovering on theirs.

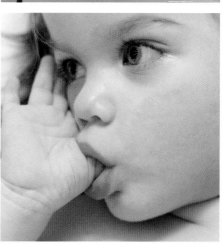

Wannabe...

Of course you've seen the pictures of famous footballers kicking a ball around as a toddler. But you didn't see the ones of them sailing, cooking, dancing and computing. The wider the selection of shots you take, the better your chances of rewriting history. Don't forget the "just like his Mum / Dad" pictures – in your football scarf, doing your hobby or wearing your uniform.

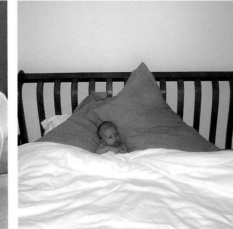

So cute

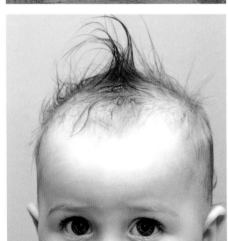

Composition ideas – for the shots that make you say "Aah." Which is probably most of them.

Spot the
difference

With or without flash

Turning off the flash gives a gentler, more flattering look, as illustrated here.

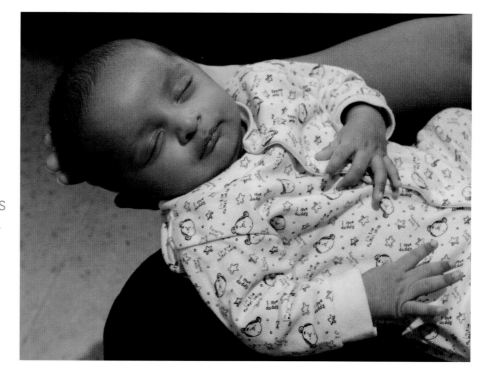

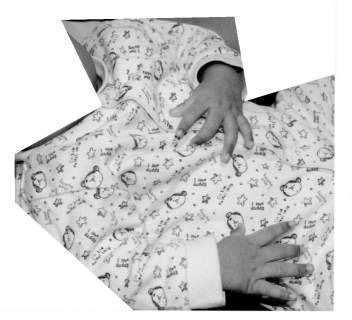

In this second image, taken with flash, there is more shine on the baby's face and a darker shadow behind his head.

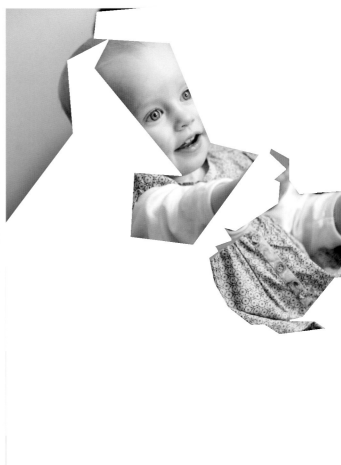

Avoiding clutter

The second shot was achieved by moving just a couple
of toys. Then the photographer moved around the child,
to ensure the remaining toys were out of shot.

Flat or side lighting

This is an appealing picture of a little girl, lit from the front.

But see how much more detail there is in her face, when lit from the side.

Taken from above or on a level

A photo taken from above will highlight the eyes and often works well, but it will always be an outsider's view of your subject. By crouching down at the child's level you are drawn into their world.

Using focus lock

Many simple cameras will focus on the dead centre of the image – which may be a point in the distance, leaving your subjects blurred.

Remember to use your focus lock, if your subjects are off centre. Centre the camera on the subject, half depress the shutter release and hold it there while you recompose, and then take, your shot.

Red eye

Avoid red eye by following the tips on page 36.
Alternatively correct it on your computer after the
event, using **post production** software.

Standing back or getting close

Step forward to avoid excess foreground in your shot. Fill the frame with your subject for a stronger image. Then take another picture from further back, in case you want to change the **crop** at a later stage.

The rule of thirds

While an image can look perfectly good with the subject dead centre, an off-centre shot will be easier on the eye. Try to place the focus of your shot (e.g. the eyes) on one of the four intersections marked with a red cross – a third of the way up, down or in from each side.

The portraiture setting

Use the portraiture setting on your camera (see page 20) to blur the background and highlight your subject, as in the first image of the little girl. But note that, with two subjects, their heads must be side by side. If one is behind the other, as in the second shot shown above, use your automatic setting to keep them both in focus.

Jargon buster

To be used tit for tat as ammunition against anyone who bores you with tales of their baby's "routine".

Ambient. Light which is already there (not provided by the photographer). "I prefer ambient lighting" means "I don't like flash" and is a cool thing to say.

Aperture. The hole in your camera the light goes through. Confusingly, a bigger number means a smaller hole and less light.

Blog. An online journal, often containing images and videos.

Bracketing. A popular DIY term. In photography it means taking several shots, with different apertures or shutter speeds to hedge your bets.

Camera shake. Moving the camera (even slightly) as you take the shot. Camera shake is the main cause of blurred images.

Catch lights. Little reflections in the eyes which make your child twinkle.

CCD. Charge Coupled Device. The bit where the image is recorded on a digital camera (the equivalent of film). Not many people know that!

Composition. The content of your picture. What's in and out.

Contrast. The difference between the light and dark parts of your picture.

Crop. The crop (noun): how much or little of the subject matter you include in the shot. To crop (verb): to chop out the bits you wish you hadn't taken in the first place.

Depth of field. How much of the shot is in focus, front to back. The 'people' or 'portraiture' setting on your camera has a short depth of field, meaning your subject stands out and the background is blurred. This is the photographic equivalent of the offside rule –

many of us have heard the term but never quite understood it.

Desaturate. Take out one or more colours, e.g. change a colour image to black and white.

Exposure. The amount of light allowed to fall on the image sensor while the image is being taken, measured in time (long or short exposure).

Face detection. Relatively new technology whereby the camera can detect where the faces are and will focus automatically on those, not the background. Some cameras can even pick out the children (child priority) and focus on them, in recognition of the fact that no-one else matters once you have a baby.

F-stop. The measurement of light able to pass through the lens of the camera. Shifting one f-stop (f/2, f/2.8 etc.) doubles or halves the light passing through the lens. A bit like the G-spot, experts use the F-stop all the time, but most of us don't need to worry about it unduly.

Fill in light. Extra light added in the foreground to lighten the shadows. Fill in light may be a flash, a lamp or a reflector and will drastically improve your shots in bright sunlight.

Flat lighting. Lighting that comes from all around (as opposed to 'directional lighting'). Flat lighting gives fewer shadows, but the shot can look a bit two-dimensional. "Unfortunately the light is a bit flat" is a good phrase to use in more or less any open space on an overcast day.

Focus lock. To lock the focus on an off centre subject, centre the camera on the subject, half depress the shutter release and hold it there while you recompose your shot. (The green box or flashing blocks indicate the area in focus.) Now press the shutter release down fully to take the picture.

Golden light. The lovely soft (golden!) light at sunrise and sunset.

High speed memory card. A high speed memory card does not reduce the delay on some cameras between pressing the button and capturing the shot. However, it does record the image to the card faster, meaning your camera is ready to shoot again more quickly.

ISO / 'film' speed / ASA. ISO is a measure of light intensity. With some digital cameras you can change the ISO picture by picture. The higher ISO (400+) is more sensitive to light, meaning you can shoot in dimmer situations without needing your flash. ISO 100 (a 'slow' film) should only really be used in bright sunlight. The disadvantage of faster film (400+) is that the shot is more grainy. If you have to choose a default film speed, go for ISO 400 (or 200 with an SLR). Use ISO 400+ if you are inside and ISO 100 only for really bright sun.

Landscape. Sideways (the natural way to hold the camera).

Leading line. A strong line across your photo which leads your eye towards (or away from) your subject. A leading line can be deliberate or accidental, helpful or disruptive.

Megapixels. One megapixel is a million pixels. The more megapixels your camera has, the bigger the potential print size. Don't assume that all pictures can be blown up to poster size. Two megapixels should suffice for a 15cm x 10cm print, but around ten megapixels are required for a good quality poster.

Model release form. A legal release granting permission to publish the photograph in one form or another.

Parallax error. With most 'point and shoot' cameras, what you see in the viewfinder or display panel is slightly different from what the lens 'sees', so you must follow the crop lines to avoid cutting off people's heads.

Portrait. Long ways. Turn the camera through 90 degrees and suddenly the head fits the frame more easily.

Post production. Playing around with your shots after you've taken them, using software such as Adobe® Photoshop®, Picasa®, Picnik® or Irfan View®. You can do some really neat stuff, but you can also miss your children growing up if you spend too long on it.

Profile. Sideways on.

Red eye. That demonic look which happens if the light bounces from the retina of the eye. As if children can't look like little devils all by themselves.

Reflector. A reflector is something white, silver or gold which can be held out of sight of the lens to reflect extra light onto your subject's face. Make your own by wrapping a white pillow case or silver baking foil around a piece of card. Alternatively buy a simple folding reflector relatively cheaply. White sheets or clothing will also reflect light.

Rule of thirds. This rule advises photographers not to stick the subject straight in the middle but to position them one third from top / bottom / sides. All very well in theory.

Self timer. Setting which gives a delay between pressing the shutter release and taking the shot – just enough time for you to run round and be in the picture yourself.

Shutter release. The button you press to take the picture.

Shutter speed. How much time the shutter is open for. Measured in fractions of one second, so a small number means the shutter is open longer. Which means you have to keep very still. As does your subject. Which is almost impossible below 1/125 of a second. The longer the shutter speed, the less need for flash light, but the more need for a tripod to stop the photo being blurred.

SLR. Single lens reflex. Posh camera where what you see through the lens is exactly what you get (no parallax error).

Story board. A sequence of pictures that make up a story.

Tripod. A three legged 'stabiliser' for your camera. Unlike your hands, a tripod can keep the camera completely still for long exposures, because it doesn't have to breathe.

TTL. Through the lens. Flash which measures the light actually hitting the film.

Wide angle lens. 35mm and under. These lenses enable you to capture the surrounding area as well as the subject. However, if you use a wide angle to take a close up, it will distort (widen) the face.

Zoom lens or long lens or telephoto lens. They are all much the same thing and allow you to get close without moving. They have a short depth of field i.e. they will focus on the subject and blur everything else. They are great for portraits but require more light, a steady hand (or a tripod) and fast 'film' speed (ISO).